CORPUS OF **MAYA**

HIEROGLYPHIC INSCRIPTIONS

VOLUME 3   PART 2   YAXCHILAN

CORPUS

OF

MAYA

HIEROGLYPHIC

INSCRIPTIONS

Volume 3   Part 2

IAN GRAHAM

Assistant Curator
of Maya Hieroglyphics
Peabody Museum, Harvard University

PEABODY MUSEUM
OF ARCHÆOLOGY AND ETHNOLOGY
HARVARD UNIVERSITY
CAMBRIDGE, MASSACHUSETTS

1979

ACKNOWLEDGMENTS

Publication of this fascicle was made possible through the generosity of:

    Mr. and Mrs. Robert S. Pirie

    Sra. Ana María Pérez de Sánchez

    Mrs. A. Murray Vaughan

Grateful acknowledgment is made to the Instituto Nacional de Antropología e Historia of Mexico for their cooperation in authorizing the necessary work at Yaxchilan and for their permission to reproduce photographs of all the sculpture in this the second part of volume 3, except for Lintel 35 and the upper half of Lintel 41; with respect to these, thanks are due to the Trustees of the British Museum for their kindness. Fieldwork and preparation of the text were carried out for the most part in the period of a three-year grant from the National Endowment for the Humanities and with the benefit of substantial contributions from the Stella and Charles Guttman Foundation of New York, from Mrs. John de Menil, and from the Bowditch Exploration Fund of the Peabody Museum, which together were matched by the Endowment.

Yaxchilan, Lintel 29

LOCATION   Central doorway of Structure 10. The lintel remained in place until about 1950, as is shown by a photograph of the doorway, misleadingly captioned, in Dana and Ginger Lamb's *Quest for the Lost City* (New York: Harper & Brothers, 1951, p. 117). At a later date a large cedar tree growing out of Structure 10 fell and demolished much of it. In 1977 the lintel was located by Graham among debris. As set over the doorway, the lintel had its right-hand edge facing outward.

CONDITION   Unbroken and well preserved.

MATERIAL   Fine-grained limestone, differing from that of Lintels 30 and 31 in not showing layers or strata of varying color.

SHAPE   The sculptured surface is flat; the sides are parallel.

DIMENSIONS	MW	0.76 m
	HSc	0.86 m
	WSc	0.60 m
	MTh	0.41 m
	Rel	0.5 cm

CARVED AREAS   Underside only.

PHOTOGRAPH   Graham, 1977.

DRAWING   Graham, based on a drawing corrected by artificial light.

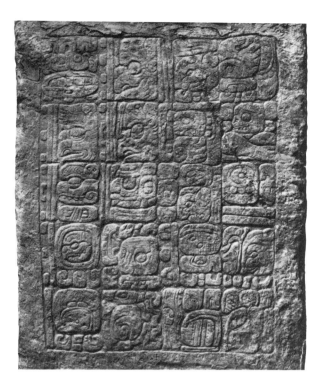

Yaxchilan, Lintel 30

LOCATION   Found by Maudslay in situ over the second doorway from the southeast end of Structure 10. The lintel had fallen by the time of Maler's first visit.

CONDITION   Unbroken and well preserved. A comparison of the lintel with Maudslay's plaster cast shows that a slight deterioration through erosion has occurred.

MATERIAL   Fine-grained limestone, noticeably striated.

SHAPE   The sculptured surface is flat; the sides are parallel.

DIMENSIONS   MW   1.04 m
            HSc   0.82 m
            WSc   0.89 m
            MTh   0.28 m
            Rel   0.5   cm

CARVED AREAS   Underside only.

PHOTOGRAPH   Graham, 1976.

DRAWING   Graham, based on a drawing corrected by artificial light and on study of Maudslay's plaster cast.

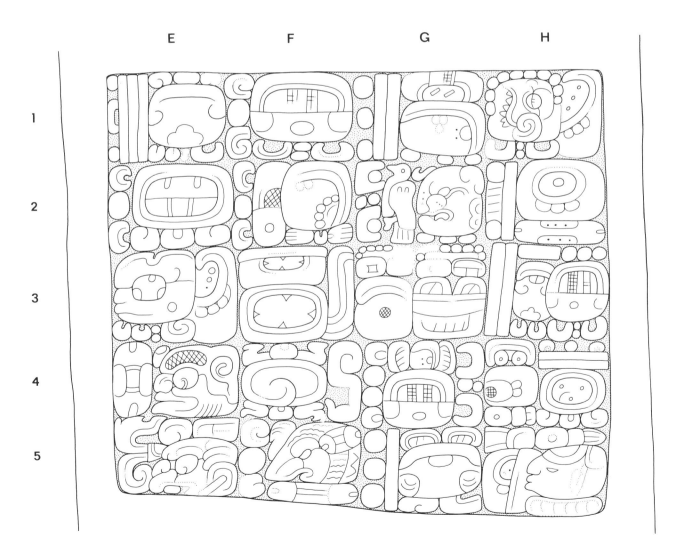

Yaxchilan, Lintel 31

LOCATION   At the time of Maudslay's and Maler's visits, the lintel was in situ over the doorway nearest the southeast end of Structure 10. It fell sometime in the first decade of the twentieth century.

CONDITION   Unbroken and fairly well preserved.

MATERIAL   Fine-grained limestone, noticeably striated.

SHAPE   The sculptured surface is flat; the sides are parallel.

DIMENSIONS   MW   1.08 m
             HSc   0.81 m
             WSc   0.95 m
             MTh   0.36 m
             Rel   0.3 cm

CARVED AREAS   Underside only.

PHOTOGRAPH   Graham, 1976.

DRAWING   Graham, based on a drawing corrected by artificial light and on study of Maler's photograph.

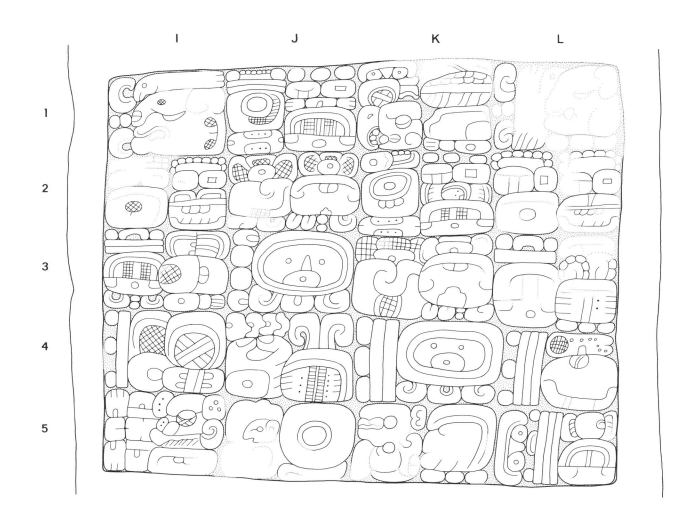

Yaxchilan, Lintel 32

LOCATION Excavated by Maler from debris in front of the middle doorway of Structure 13. Removed in 1964 to the Museo Nacional de Antropología, Mexico City.

CONDITION Unbroken and well preserved when found. Subsequent to its discovery considerable erosion took place.

MATERIAL Fine-grained limestone.

SHAPE The sculptured surface is flat; the sides are parallel.

DIMENSIONS

MW	0.59	m
HSc	0.81	m
WSc	0.53	m
MTh	0.27	m
Rel	0.5	cm

CARVED AREAS Underside only.

PHOTOGRAPH Graham, 1975.

DRAWING Graham, based on a drawing corrected by artificial light and on study of Maler's photograph and the photograph of a cast from a mold made by him.

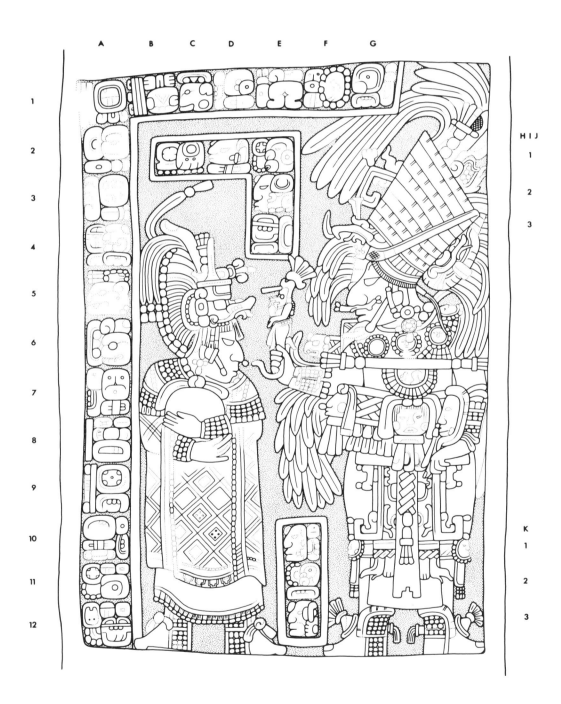

Yaxchilan, Lintel 33

LOCATION Found by Maler among debris in front of the northeastern doorway of Structure 13. Removed in 1964 to the Museo Nacional de Antropología, Mexico City.

CONDITION Broken into two pieces when found, but otherwise fairly well preserved, and showing red paint in several places. Some loss of detail has since occurred.

MATERIAL Fine-grained limestone.

SHAPE The sculptured surface is flat; the sides are somewhat convergent toward the bottom.

DIMENSIONS MW   0.71 m
            HSc   0.81 m
            WSc   0.61 m
            MTh   0.32 m
            Rel   0.9 cm

CARVED AREAS   Underside only.

PHOTOGRAPHS   Graham, 1975.

DRAWING   Graham, based on a drawing corrected by artificial light, on Maler's photograph, and on the cast from a mold made by him.

Stereophotos

Yaxchilan, Lintel 34

LOCATION   Found by Maler broken and partly fallen from its setting over the southwesternmost doorway of Structure 12. The triangular upper fragment was still in place in 1975. Two other fragments are in storage at Yaxchilan, and a third, the bottom fragment, may be there too. A red-painted limestone fragment in the Peabody Museum (Cat. No. C-3945), which is carved in relief with one almost complete glyph and part of another, can be ascribed without doubt to this lintel. In view of the regret expressed by Maler (1903, p. 133) over the loss of other fragments of this lintel, it is evident that he sent this one to the Peabody Museum to ensure its preservation.

CONDITION   Broken into five known pieces and others now lost. The upper part and the Peabody Museum fragment are in pristine condition and retain their red paint. Part of the middle fragment was already badly eroded when photographed by Morley in 1931.

MATERIAL   Fine-grained limestone.

SHAPE   The sculptured surface is flat, and the sides seem to have been parallel.

DIMENSIONS   MW   0.65 m
              HSc   unknown
              WSc   0.55 m (approx.)
              MTh   not measured
              Rel   0.4 cm

CARVED AREAS   Underside only.

PHOTOGRAPH   Graham, 1975.

DRAWING   Graham, based on a drawing corrected by artificial light.

NOTE   The positioning of the Peabody Museum fragment at D2 in the drawing is conjectural and not supported by a mating of surfaces. In his field journal for April 17, 1931 (Peabody Museum Archives), Morley describes clearing debris down to floor level in this doorway and finding two small fragments, both fitting the north, or upper, end of the lintel. No photograph or drawing of these seems to exist, nor have the fragments come to light.

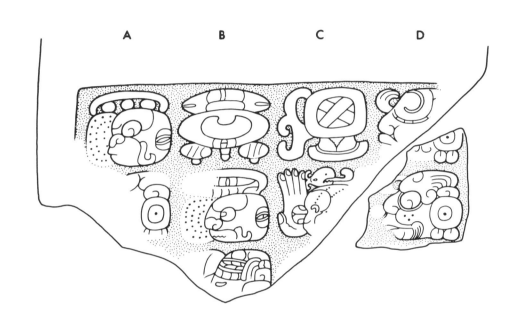

Yaxchilan, Lintel 35

LOCATION   Found by Maudslay in 1882 among debris in front of the third doorway from the northeastern end of Structure 12. The carved surface was sawn off in the following year on Maudslay's orders and is now in the British Museum.

CONDITION   Intact when found, but during or after the sawing, the top of the panel, carrying the first row of glyphs, broke off and then broke in half. The left-hand border of the panel has been sawn off too. The condition of the carved surface is pristine, with red paint remaining near the top and the bottom of the panel.

MATERIAL   Fine-grained limestone.

SHAPE   The sculptured surface is very flat; the sides are parallel.

DIMENSIONS
MW	0.63 m	(trimmed)
HSc	0.97 m	
WSc	0.57 m	
MTh	unknown	
Rel	0.6 cm	

CARVED AREAS   Underside only.

PHOTOGRAPH   Graham, 1974.

DRAWING   Graham, based on a drawing corrected by artificial light.

NOTE   Morley's naming of the glyph columns on five of the seven lintels of Structure 12 as a single series, from A to X, has been discarded. Each lintel is here lettered separately. The following is a concordance between Morley's lettering (cited first) and that employed here:

U	A
V	B
W	C
X	D

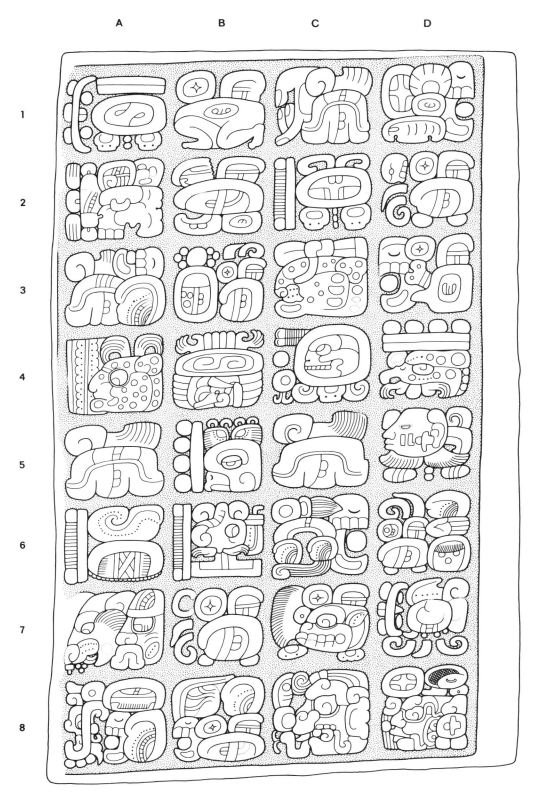

Yaxchilan, Lintel 36

LOCATION First mentioned by Maler, the lintel lies near the central doorway of the seven in the facade of Structure 12.

CONDITION Unbroken, but severely eroded.

MATERIAL Fine-grained limestone.

SHAPE The sculptured surface appears to have been flat, and the sides parallel.

DIMENSIONS
MW	0.65 m	
HSc	0.99 m	
WSc	0.56 m	
MTh	0.24 m	
Rel	0.3	cm (approx.)

CARVED AREAS Underside only.

PHOTOGRAPH Morley, 1931.

Yaxchilan, Lintel 37

LOCATION   Found by Maudslay in 1882, buried in debris in front of the second doorway from the northeastern end of Structure 12. The lintel was seen by Morley during his 1931 visit to Yaxchilan (field notes on inscriptions, vol. 12, pp. 159 and 166, Peabody Museum Archives), but it has not been located by the author.

CONDITION   Intact when discovered, and in pristine condition, still showing red paint.

MATERIAL   Presumably limestone, although there is no documentation on this point.

SHAPE   The photograph and plaster cast suggest that the lintel was as carefully and accurately dressed as others in the same building.

DIMENSIONS

MW	0.70	m
HSc	0.93	m
WSc	0.57	m
MTh	unknown	
Rel	0.6	cm

CARVED AREAS   Underside only.

PHOTOGRAPH   Maudslay (of plaster cast).

DRAWING   Graham, based on Maler's photograph and on Maudslay's plaster cast (British Museum).

NOTE   Morley's designation of the glyph columns on five of the seven lintels of Structure 12 as a single series, running from A to X, has been discarded. Each lintel is here lettered separately. The following is a concordance between Morley's lettering (cited first) and that employed here:

U	A
V	B
W	C
X	D

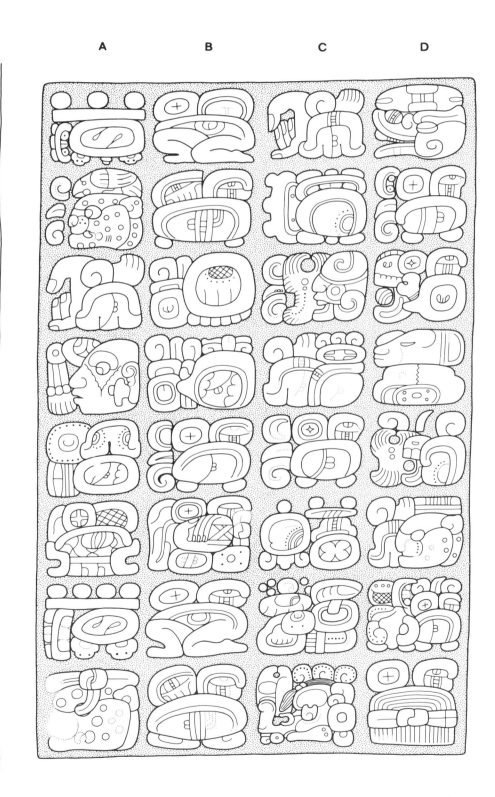

Yaxchilan, Lintel 38

LOCATION Discovered by Maler in 1900 in situ, but buried in debris, in front of the southwestern doorway of Structure 16, where it still lies.

CONDITION Intact, with its sculptured surface fairly well preserved when discovered, although subsequently it has suffered some further erosion.

MATERIAL Fine-grained limestone.

SHAPE A carefully dressed slab, except that its thickness is not quite uniform.

DIMENSIONS
MW	0.97	m
HSc	0.26	m
WSc	1.26	m
MTh	0.32	m
Rel	0.7	cm

CARVED AREAS Front edge only.

PHOTOGRAPH Reproduced from Maler's original negative.

DRAWING Graham, based on a drawing corrected by artificial light and on Maler's photograph.

NOTE Morley notes that Maler transposed the photographs of Lintels 38 and 40 in his report (1903, pl. LXV).

Yaxchilan, Lintel 39

LOCATION Discovered by Maler in 1900, buried in debris, having slipped from the jambs of the central doorway of Structure 16. It was removed in 1964 to the Museo Nacional de Antropología, Mexico City.

CONDITION Intact, with its sculptured surface very well preserved when discovered; some further erosion is now evident.

SHAPE The slab is well dressed, although its thickness is not uniform.

DIMENSIONS

MW	0.98 m	(underside)
HSc	0.25 m	
WSc	1.22 m	
MTh	0.32 m	
Rel	0.8 cm	

CARVED AREAS Front edge only.

PHOTOGRAPH Reproduced from Maler's original negative.

DRAWING Graham, based on a drawing corrected by artificial light and on Maler's photograph.

Yaxchilan, Lintel 40

LOCATION   Discovered by Maler in 1897 in situ over the northeastern doorway of Structure 16.

CONDITION   Intact and fairly well preserved except in certain areas.

MATERIAL   Fine-grained limestone containing some flaws.

SHAPE   The slab is accurately cut with parallel sides and a rectangular cross section.

DIMENSIONS   MW   0.95 m
HSc   0.25 m
WSc   1.26 m
MTh   0.32 m
Rel   0.5 cm

CARVED AREAS   Front edge only.

PHOTOGRAPH   Graham, 1973.

DRAWING   Graham, based on a drawing corrected by artificial light and on study of Maler's plaster cast.

NOTE   Morley notes that Maler transposed the photographs of Lintels 38 and 40 in his report (1903, pl. LXV). The photograph used there to illustrate Lintel 40 actually shows the plaster cast.

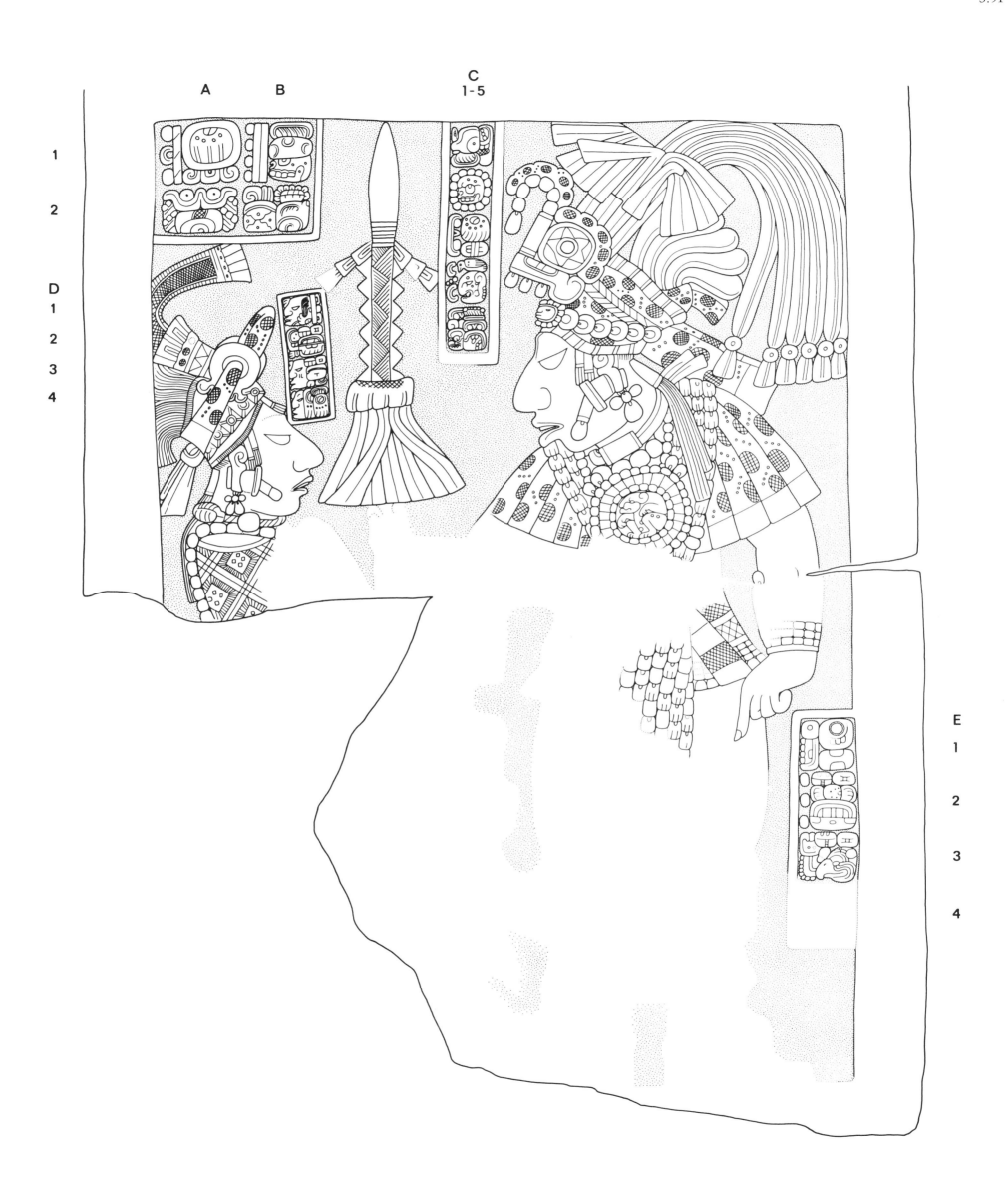

LOCATION The upper half of the lintel was discovered by Maudslay in 1882 in front of the south doorway of Structure 42. Four years later the carved surface was sawn off by Gorgonio López acting on Maudslay's instructions and removed to England. It is now in the British Museum. The incomplete lower portion seems to have been lying close by, partly exposed and with its carved surface uppermost. This piece was first examined and photographed by Morley in 1931.

CONDITION Broken into two large pieces and others not yet found. The upper portion is in pristine condition; at the time of discovery, the relief on the lower portion had been largely effaced, although an area on the right-hand side, presumably protected from weathering by debris, remained in good condition.

MATERIAL Fine-grained limestone.

SHAPE The sculptured surface is flat; the sides are seemingly parallel.

DIMENSIONS

MW	0.93 m	
HSc	1.15 m (approx.)	
WSc	0.76 m	
MTh	0.34 m	
Rel	1.6 cm	

CARVED AREAS Underside only.

PHOTOGRAPH Composite: upper portion, Graham, 1974; lower portion, Morley, 1931.

DRAWING Graham, based on drawings corrected by artificial light.

Yaxchilan, Lintel 42

LOCATION   Discovered in situ over the middle doorway of Structure 42 by Maudslay in 1882.

CONDITION   Intact, save for losses along the left-hand (outer) edge. The surface of the sculpture is in almost pristine condition, except for some losses by flaking, notably in the upper glyph panel. There has been no detectable deterioration since the piece was discovered and recorded by the making of a plaster cast (now in the British Museum).

MATERIAL   Fine-grained limestone of a yellowish color.

SHAPE   The sculptured surface is flat, and the sides are parallel.

DIMENSIONS
MW	0.98	m
HSc	1.08	m
WSc	0.84	m
MTh	0.33	m
Rel	0.7	cm

CARVED AREAS   Underside only.

PHOTOGRAPH   Graham, 1974. Because rubble half-filled the doorway, it was impossible to cover the whole sculptured area in a single photograph. A mosaic of four detail photographs is reproduced here.

DRAWING   Graham, based on a drawing corrected by artificial light. The initial tracing was done from a photograph of Maudslay's cast, rather than from the author's mosaic photograph, in order to avoid distortion inherent in the latter.

LOCATION Discovered in the north doorway of Structure 42 by Maudslay in 1882. The upper part was lying in the doorway, while the lower part was still in situ. Both pieces were removed in 1964 to the Museo Nacional de Antropología, Mexico City.

CONDITION Broken into two large pieces when discovered; other small fragments have yet to be found. The sculptured surface is very well preserved and has suffered negligible erosion since its discovery.

Comparison of the lintel with Maudslay's cast and Maler's photograph, however, does disclose a few very small losses by breakage, notably portions of glyphs A1 and D7.

MATERIAL Very fine-grained limestone.

SHAPE The sculptured surface is flat, and the sides are parallel.

DIMENSIONS

MW	0.92 m
HSc	1.09 m
WSc	0.77 m
MTh	0.30 m
Rel	1.8 cm

CARVED AREAS Underside only.

PHOTOGRAPHS Graham, 1974.

DRAWING Graham, based on a drawing corrected by artificial light and on Maudslay's plaster cast (now in the British Museum) and Maler's photograph.

Stereophotos

Yaxchilan, Lintel 44

LOCATION   The lintel, which spans the southeast doorway of Structure 44, must have been seen by Maudslay, but Maler was the first to make mention of it. Two important fragments constituting about one quarter of the lintel were excavated by Karl Ruppert in 1931 from debris in the doorway.

CONDITION   Broken into five main fragments, three of which remain in situ, and other smaller pieces never found. Much of the sculptured surface toward the outer (right-hand) edge has been damaged, perhaps by fire, as Maler plausibly suggested. Elsewhere details of the sculpture are well preserved.

MATERIAL   Very fine-grained limestone.

SHAPE   As far as can be determined the lintel was carefully hewn, although the sides are not parallel but converge toward the top.

DIMENSIONS   MW   0.98 m
             HSc   0.98 m
             WSc   0.84 m (approx.)
             MTh   0.30 m
             Rel   2.0 cm

CARVED AREAS   Underside only.

PHOTOGRAPH   Graham, 1975.

DRAWING   Graham, based on a drawing corrected by artificial light.

NOTE   Morley designated the glyph columns on the lintels and hieroglyphic steps of Structure 44 as a single series, running from A to J''. His scheme is presented graphically in *The Inscriptions of Peten* (Morley 1937–38, fig. 27). In the present work each lintel has its glyph columns lettered separately. The single column on this lintel, here called A, was given the letter L' by Morley.

Yaxchilan, Lintel 45

LOCATION   In situ over the middle doorway of Structure 44, where it was discovered by Maudslay in 1882. A mold was taken at that time, a cast from which is in the British Museum.

CONDITION   Cracked through, with losses along both edges above this crack. The sculptured surface has been destroyed by flaking in some areas; in others it remains in excellent condition. Traces of red paint remain.

MATERIAL   Very fine-grained limestone.

SHAPE   The sculptured surface is flat; the sides are parallel.

DIMENSIONS
MW	1.07	m
HSc	0.92	m
WSc	0.92	m
MTh	0.24	m
Rel	2.1	cm

CARVED AREAS Underside only.

PHOTOGRAPHS Graham, 1975.

DRAWINGS Graham, based on a drawing corrected by artificial light.

NOTE Morley designated the glyph columns on the lintels and hieroglyphic steps of Structure 44 as a single series running from A to J''. His scheme is presented graphically in *The Inscriptions of Peten* (Morley 1937–38, fig. 27). In the present work each lintel has its glyph columns lettered separately. The following is a concordance between Morley's lettering (cited first) and that employed here:

R	A
S	B
T	C
U	D

Details

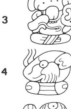

Yaxchilan, Lintel 46

LOCATION   In situ over the northwest doorway of Structure 44, where it was first seen by Maudslay in 1882.

CONDITION   Cracked into five large pieces and one small one, all precariously in situ at the time of discovery. Other small fragments were never found. The large central piece fell sometime between Maler's third visit (1900) and Morley's of 1931. Much of the surface has been destroyed, perhaps by fire; elsewhere it remains in excellent condition, with red paint still in evidence.

MATERIAL   Very fine-grained limestone.

SHAPE   The sculptured surface is flat; the sides are parallel.

DIMENSIONS

MW	1.04 m
HSc	0.96 m (approx.)
WSc	unknown
MTh	0.26 m
Rel	1.7 cm

CARVED AREAS   Underside only.

PHOTOGRAPHS   Graham, 1973 and 1974. The whole design is shown at the usual scale of 1:10 in a photograph of Maudslay's plaster cast in the British Museum. The detail photographs are of the original.

DRAWINGS   Graham, based on a drawing corrected by artificial light, the cast having been studied as well as the original.

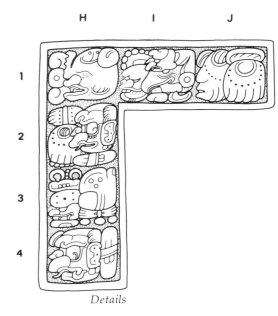

Details

NOTE Morley designated the glyph columns on the lintels and hieroglyphic steps
of Structure 44 as a single series, running
from A to J''. His scheme is presented
graphically in *The Inscriptions of Peten*
(Morley 1937–38, fig. 27). As the column
letters allocated by him for this lintel began
with A'', the lintel-by-lintel nomenclature
employed in the present work for this
structure involves simply the suppression
of the double prime: thus A, B, C, etc.,
instead of A'', B'', C''.

Details

Details

Yaxchilan, Lintel 47

LOCATION Discovered in 1931 in front of the second doorway from the southwest end of Structure 12. In 1964 this lintel was removed to the Museo Nacional de Antropología, Mexico City.

CONDITION When found, this lintel was broken into two large and several smaller pieces. The sculptured surface had suffered only slight erosion. No further erosion occurred prior to its removal, but three small fragments carrying portions of glyphs A3, A8, and D2 have been lost. Red paint remains on the lower border.

MATERIAL Fine-grained limestone.

SHAPE The sculptured surface is very flat, and the sides are parallel.

DIMENSIONS

MW	0.68	m
HSc	0.97	m
WSc	0.55	m
MTh	0.25	m
Rel	0.7	cm

CARVED AREAS Underside only.

PHOTOGRAPHS Graham, 1974.

DRAWING Graham, based on a drawing corrected by artificial light and on Morley's 1931 photograph.

NOTE Morley's designation of the glyph columns on five of the seven lintels of Structure 12 as a single series, running from A to X, has been discarded. Each lintel is here lettered separately. The following is a concordance between Morley's lettering (cited first) and that employed here:

E	A
F	B
G	C
H	D

Stereophotos

Stereophotos

Yaxchilan, Lintel 48

LOCATION Discovered by Karl Ruppert in 1931 in debris in front of the third doorway from the southwestern end of Structure 12. Removed in 1964 to the Museo Nacional de Antropología, Mexico City.

CONDITION Two main pieces are known; part of the sculpture is missing. One small fragment, part of the ISIG, that is seen in Morley's photograph has since disappeared, and another, part of the *baktun* coefficient, is mentioned by Morley

(1937–38, vol. 2, p. 369, note 68). The surface was in pristine state when found, with red paint in the grooves, as noted by Morley (field journal, April 17, 1931, Peabody Museum Archives). A very slight degree of erosion has since occurred.

MATERIAL Very fine-grained limestone.

SHAPE The sculptured surface is flat; the sides are parallel.

DIMENSIONS MW   0.67 m
HSc   0.98 m
WSc   0.55 m
MTh   0.23 m
Rel   0.7 cm

CARVED AREAS Underside only.

PHOTOGRAPHS Graham, 1973.

DRAWING Graham, based on a drawing corrected by artificial light and on Morley's 1931 photograph.

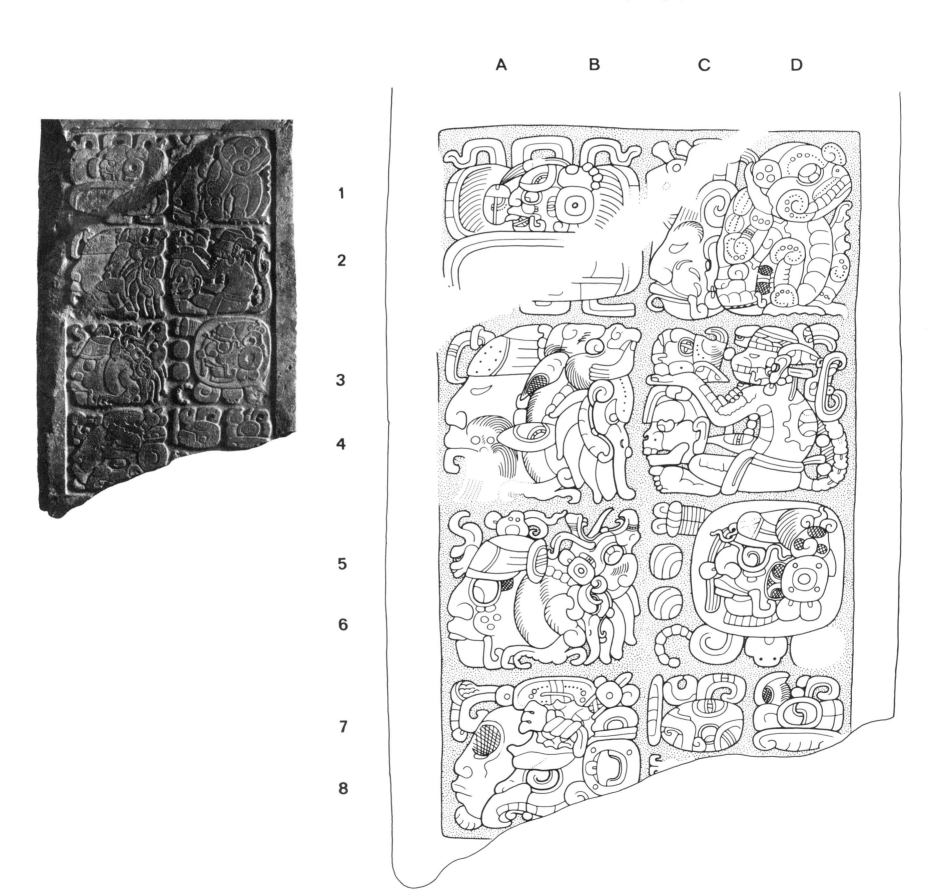

Stereophotos

Yaxchilan, Lintel 49

LOCATION   Discovered in 1931 in front of the last doorway toward the northeast in the line of seven doorways in the facade of Structure 12.

CONDITION   When found, the lintel was broken into four large and several smaller pieces, many of which were not located, with the consequent loss of most of column A of the inscription. In 1972 Graham found three more small fragments bearing portions of glyphs A1, A5, and A6, but part of A2 had been broken off and could not be found. Traces of red paint remain.

MATERIAL   Fine-grained limestone.

SHAPE   The sculptured surface is very flat; the sides were probably parallel.

DIMENSIONS

MW	0.66	m
HSc	0.97	m
WSc	0.55	m
MTh	0.25	m
Rel	0.4	cm

CARVED AREAS   Underside only.

PHOTOGRAPH   Graham, 1973.

DRAWING   Graham, based on a drawing corrected by artificial light and on Morley's 1931 photograph.

NOTE   Morley's designation of the glyph columns on five of the seven lintels of Structure 12 as a single series, running from A to X, has been discarded. Each lintel is here lettered separately. The following is a concordance between Morley's lettering (cited first) and that employed here:

M	A
N	B
O	C
P	D

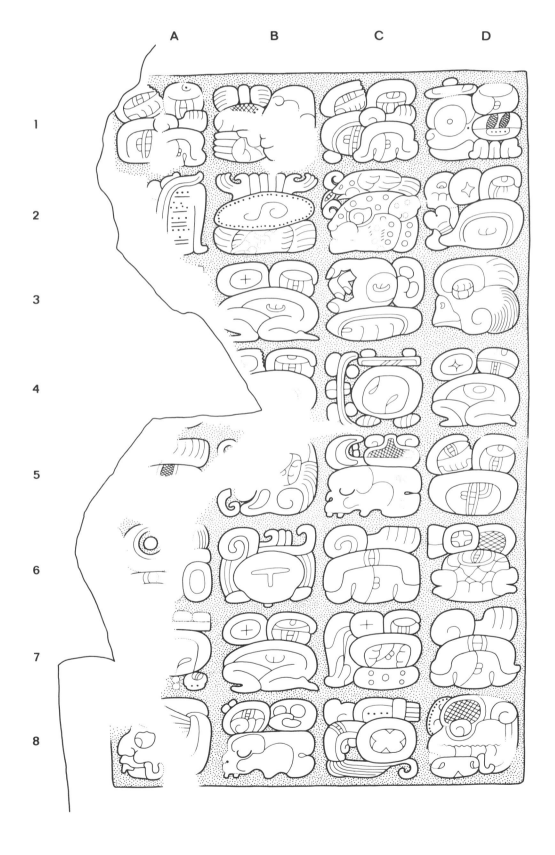

Yaxchilan, Lintel 50

LOCATION   Found by Karl Ruppert in 1931 in debris in front of the southwestern doorway of Structure 13.

CONDITION   Unbroken. The condition of the sculptured surface ranges from moderately good to poor.

MATERIAL   Limestone flawed by holes.

SHAPE   The sculptured surface is generally flat, although uneven. The sides are parallel.

DIMENSIONS

MW	0.68	m
HSc	0.59	m
WSc	0.58	m
MTh	0.23	m
Rel	0.3	cm

CARVED AREAS   Underside only.

PHOTOGRAPH   Morley, 1931.

DRAWING   Graham, based on a field drawing not corrected by artificial light and on Morley's photographs.

Yaxchilan, Lintel 51

LOCATION   Found lying face down in front of the east doorway of Structure 55 by John Bolles in 1931.

CONDITION   Unbroken. The condition of the sculptured surface was moderately good near the bottom of the design and very poor near the top.

MATERIAL   Limestone of poor quality, crisscrossed with fissures.

SHAPE   The sculptured surface is flat; the sides are parallel.

DIMENSIONS   MW   0.91 m
              HSc   0.82 m
              WSc   0.76 m
              MTh   0.30 m
              Rel   1.0 cm

CARVED AREAS   Underside only.

PHOTOGRAPH   Graham, 1978.

DRAWING   Graham, based on a drawing corrected by artificial light and on Morley's 1931 photograph.

Yaxchilan, Lintel 52

LOCATION   Found lying face down in front of the middle doorway of Structure 55 by John Bolles in 1931.

CONDITION   Unbroken as regards the sculptured area. The surface was well preserved when found, but subsequently it has suffered considerable erosion.

MATERIAL   Limestone of fine grain, though not free of holes and fissures.

SHAPE   The sculptured surface is flat; the sides are nearly parallel, the right-hand edge being smoothly dressed, the left-hand quite uneven. The width of the lintel is considerably greater at its upper than at its lower, sculptured, surface.

DIMENSIONS
MW	0.90	m
HSc	0.92	m
WSc	0.71	m
MTh	0.25	m
Rel	1.5	cm

CARVED AREAS   Underside only.

PHOTOGRAPH   Morley, 1931.

DRAWING   Graham, based on a drawing corrected by artificial light and on Morley's photograph.

Yaxchilan, Lintel 53

LOCATION   Found lying face down in front of the west doorway of Structure 55 by John Bolles in 1931. Removed in 1964 to the Museo Nacional de Antropología, Mexico City.

CONDITION   Broken with a clean break into two pieces when found. The sculptured surface was very well preserved, although patches of harder material stained brown by iron content, that presumably once were flush with the surface, suggest by their protuberance some degree of general erosion. A further slight degradation of detail has occurred since the lintel was photographed in the year of its discovery.

MATERIAL   Fine-grained limestone.

SHAPE   The sculptured surface is flat; the sides are parallel.

DIMENSIONS
MW	0.88 m
HSc	0.92 m
WSc	0.75 m
MTh	0.24 m
Rel	1.4 cm

CARVED AREAS   Underside only.

PHOTOGRAPH   Graham, 1974.

DRAWING   Graham, based on a drawing corrected by artificial light and on Morley's 1931 photograph.

NOTE   It appears that the bundle held by the left-hand figure was originally incised with a design, probably a glyph, and that this was deliberately effaced in antiquity.

3:116

Yaxchilan, Lintel 54

LOCATION   When found by John Bolles in 1931 the lintel lay in front of the central doorway of Structure 54. In 1964 it was removed to the Museo Nacional de Antropología, Mexico City.

CONDITION   Broken in half when found, with a triangular fragment missing from the left-hand edge of the break and with small losses from glyphs B2 and H. Since then some general erosion has occurred, along with further small losses along the fracture.

MATERIAL   Fine-grained limestone.

SHAPE   The sculptured surface is flat; the sides are parallel.

DIMENSIONS   MW   0.77 m
HSc   0.97 m
WSc   0.67 m
MTh   0.31 m
Rel   1.5 cm

CARVED AREAS   Underside only.

PHOTOGRAPH   Graham, 1974.

DRAWING   Graham, based on a drawing corrected by artificial light and on Morley's 1931 photograph.

Yaxchilan, Lintel 55

LOCATION The lintel was found in 1933 or 1934 partly in situ over the central doorway of Structure 88, by Ulíses de la Cruz, the caretaker of the site. It was removed in 1964 to the Museo Nacional de Antropología, Mexico City.

CONDITION Intact and only moderately affected by weathering. Much of the plaster employed to fill imperfections in the stone is still in place; about half of the apron of the left-hand figure is modeled in plaster.

MATERIAL Hard and fine-grained limestone, extensively flawed.

SHAPE The sculptured surface is nearly flat; the sides converge slightly toward the top. The right-hand edge is somewhat better trimmed than the other and therefore may have faced outward.

DIMENSIONS

MW	1.00	m
HSc	0.60	m
WSc	0.80	m
MTh	0.20	m
Rel	0.9	cm

CARVED AREAS Underside only.

PHOTOGRAPH Graham, 1975.

DRAWING Graham, based on a drawing corrected by artificial light and on Satterthwaite's 1934 photograph.

LOCATION The lintel probably was discovered by Gorgonio López in 1886, when he returned to Yaxchilan at Maudslay's behest. Almost certainly the lintel came from a doorway in Structure 11; the shaft believed to correspond to the sawn-off edge now lies on the northeast side of Structure 74, not far from its east corner (see Part 1 of this volume, pp. 3:8 and 3:9). The sculptured edge was then sent by mistake to the Museum für Völkerkunde in Berlin. Fortunately, the museum made a plaster cast (now in the British Museum) for Maudslay, as the original was destroyed by bombing during the Second World War.

CONDITION Well preserved when found.

MATERIAL Limestone.

SHAPE The supposed carcass of this lintel has parallel edges.

DIMENSIONS
MW	0.80 m (approx.)	
HSc	0.27 m	
WSc	1.57 m	
MTh	0.38 m	
Rel	0.9 cm	

CARVED AREAS Front edge only.

PHOTOGRAPH Maudslay (of plaster cast).

DRAWING Graham, based on a drawing of the plaster cast corrected by artificial light.

Yaxchilan, Lintel 57

LOCATION   Found by Linton Satter-thwaite, Jr., in 1935 buried beneath debris in front of the east doorway of Structure 54.

CONDITION   Unbroken; its surface generally is well preserved. Some erosion has occurred since discovery.

MATERIAL   Limestone flawed by large holes, several of which still contain stucco filling.

SHAPE   The surface is fairly flat; the sides are parallel.

DIMENSIONS   MW   0.75 m
             HSc   0.91 m*
             WSc   0.63 m
             MTh   0.28 m
             Rel   1.4 cm
         *neglecting the projecting glyph

CARVED AREAS   Underside only.

PHOTOGRAPHS   Graham, 1978.

DRAWING   Graham, based on a drawing corrected by artificial light and on Satter-thwaite's 1935 photograph.

Stereophotos

Yaxchilan, Lintel 58

LOCATION   Found by Linton Satter-thwaite, Jr., in 1935 buried beneath debris where the west door of Structure 54 had been. Removed in 1964 to the Museo Nacional de Antropología, Mexico City.

CONDITION   Unbroken; its sculptured surface is very well preserved except in a few areas. Since excavation, a slight loss of detail has occurred through erosion.

MATERIAL   Limestone of good quality.

SHAPE   The sculptured surface is fairly flat; the sides are parallel.

DIMENSIONS   MW   0.75 m
HSc   0.96 m
WSc   0.66 m
MTh   0.22 m
Rel   1.0   cm

CARVED AREAS   Underside only.

PHOTOGRAPH   Graham, 1974.

DRAWING   Graham, based on a drawing corrected by artificial light and on Satter-thwaite's 1935 photograph.

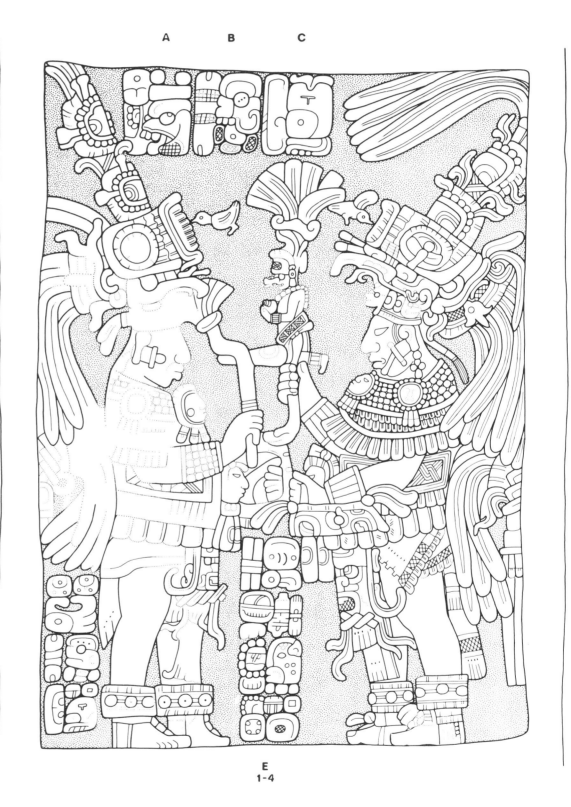